Firefighter

Angela Royston

Raintree

Raintree is an imprint of Capstone Global Library Limited, a company incorporated in England and Wales having its registered office at 7 Pilgrim Street, London, EC4V 6LB – Registered company number: 6695582

www.raintreepublishers.co.uk
myorders@raintreepublishers.co.uk

Text © Capstone Global Library Limited 2014
First published in hardback in 2014
The moral rights of the proprietor have been asserted.

Edited by Daniel Nunn, Rebecca Rissman, and Catherine Veitch
Designed by Cynthia Della-Rovere
Picture research by Ruth Blair
Production by Victoria Fitzgerald
Originated by Capstone Global Library Ltd
Printed and bound in China by South China Printing Company Ltd

ISBN 978 1 406 26067 0 (hardback)
17 16 15 14 13
10 9 8 7 6 5 4 3 2 1

ISBN 978 1 406 26074 8 (paperback)
18 17 16 15 14
10 9 8 7 6 5 4 3 2 1

British Library Cataloguing in Publication Data
Royston, Angela.
Diary of a firefighter.
363.3'7-dc23
A full catalogue record for this book is available from the British Library.

Acknowledgements
We would like to thank the following for permission to reproduce photographs: Corbis pp. 6 (© Creasource), 7 (© George Hall), 9 (© Julien Thomazo/Photononstop), 17 (© John O'Boyle/Star Ledger), 20 (© Andrew Aitchison/In Pictures), 22 (© Ramin Talaie), 25 (© Stan Carroll/ZUMA Press), 26 (© Uden Graham/Redlink), 5; Getty Images pp. 4 (Peter Macdiarmid), 12 (Jac Depczyk), 14 (YURI CORTEZ/AFP), 15 (Alain Le Bot), 16 (Adam Berry); Shutterstock pp. title page (© L Barnwell), contents page (© John Kasawa), 8 (© PerseoMedusa), 13 (© Brian McDonald), 18 (© Andreev Alexey), 19 (© TFoxFoto), 21 (© Taras Kolomiyets), 28 (© FWStudio); Superstock pp. 10 (Radius), 11 (Stockbroker / Purestock), 23, 24 (imagebroker.net), 27 (Ambient Images Inc.).

Background and design features reproduced with permission of Shutterstock. Cover photograph of firefighter next to fire reproduced with permission of Shutterstock (© Digital Storm).

We would like to thank Mark Oddi for his invaluable help in the preparation of this book.

Every effort has been made to contact copyright holders of material reproduced in this book. Any omissions will be rectified in subsequent printings if notice is given to the publisher.

All the Internet addresses (URLs) given in this book were valid at the time of going to press. However, due to the dynamic nature of the Internet, some addresses may have changed, or sites may have changed or ceased to exist since publication. While the author and publisher regret any inconvenience this may cause readers, no responsibility for any such changes can be accepted by either the author or the publisher.

Some words are shown in bold, **like this**. You can find out what they mean by looking in the Glossary.

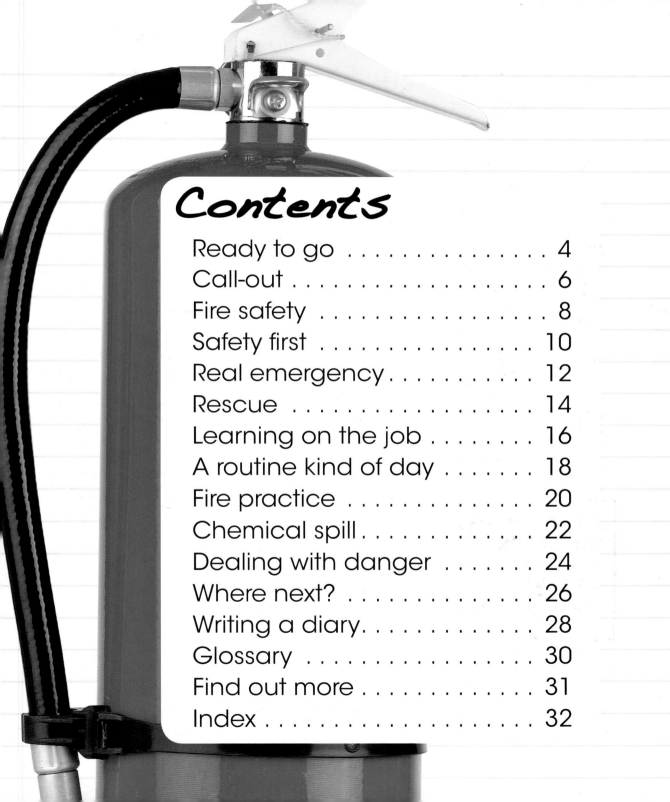

Contents

Ready to go

Monday 2 October

My days as a firefighter are so different that I've decided to keep a diary. I'm in the **fire station** now, drinking a cup of coffee – but I'm ready if the alarm goes.

I always work with the same group of firefighters. When we came on duty this morning, we checked the fire engine and all the equipment. We know that everything is in order.

Call-out

As I was writing in my diary, the alarm went off! Quick as a flash, I slid down the pole and climbed into the fire engine. I put on my hat and jacket as we raced to the fire.

When we got there, we found it was a
false alarm. We went into the building and
checked every room carefully. Someone had
seen smoke, but nothing was burning.

7

Fire safety

Tuesday 3 October

A big part of my job is preventing fires. This morning I visited a restaurant to check that it is safe. We checked the kitchen, the **fire doors**, and the **fire exits**.

This sign points to the fire exit.

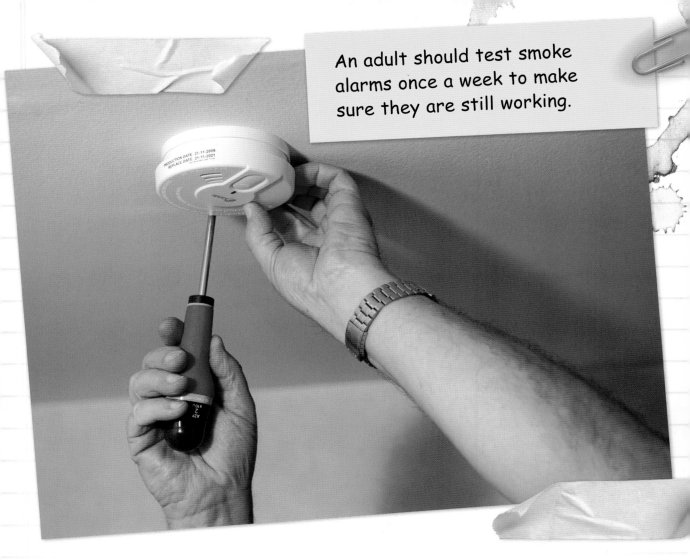

An adult should test smoke alarms once a week to make sure they are still working.

I also tested the **smoke alarms** on each floor, and made sure they were fixed in the right places. Smoke alarms beep loudly as soon as any smoke reaches them. They let people know that they have to get out.

Safety first

Safety is the most important part of our job. We save people before we worry about property. We keep ourselves safe, too. Our clothes are made of special material that does not catch fire.

helmet

breathing apparatus

fire resistant material

We use **breathing apparatus** whenever we go into a burning building. It gives us clean air to breathe and protects us from smoke and gases.

Real emergency

Wednesday 4 October

We had a real emergency call-out today. A mother and child were trapped in a burning flat. The **sirens** screeched as we raced through the traffic.

We could see the flames even before we arrived. I got the hose out and started spraying the flames. Then several other fire engines arrived.

Rescue

Two of our firefighters went into the building and up to the flat. There was smoke everywhere, but they managed to find the woman and the child.

By this time the long ladder was in place. Five minutes later the two **casualties** were on the ground safe and sound. It took much longer to put the fire out!

Learning on the job

Thursday 5 October

A new **recruit** called Sharon joined us at the station today. She has already trained at the Fire and Rescue Centre, so she knows how to use the equipment.

A firefighter practises rescuing a dummy person.

Meeting her made me remember my first day at the **fire station**. I couldn't wait to put what I'd learned into practice! My very first call-out was to help pump floodwater out of a basement.

A routine kind of day

Friday 6 October

Sharon, the new **recruit**, came with me to visit a school this morning. I told the children how to keep themselves safe from fire.

I told the children never to play with matches.

Sharon told them about her training, and how firefighters need to have a **good head for heights**. They also have to be good at talking to people. She's very good – the children loved her!

Fire practice

In the afternoon, we practised a **fire drill**. We do drills all the time. We get to know them so well, we do not have to stop and think in an emergency.

Then we had a session called "know your streets". This was helpful for Sharon. We went through all the local hazards we knew about, such as old, empty buildings.

Chemical spill

Saturday 7 October

We had another big call-out today. A lorry carrying barrels of dangerous **chemicals** crashed on the motorway. Some of the chemicals spilled across the road.

We put on special **hazard suits** to protect ourselves from the chemicals.

Police and fire crews were already there when we arrived. They had **cordoned off** the road and stopped the traffic. We wore **breathing apparatus** to protect us from breathing in any chemicals.

Dealing with danger

Dealing with **chemicals** and other hazards takes lots of special training. Chemicals can be dangerous to people and the environment.

This special sprayer gets our suits really clean!

We cleaned up the spill and made the rest of the barrels safe. Then our suits were washed down. We had to make sure there were no dangerous chemicals on our clothes.

Where next?

Sunday 8 October

I had a day off at last, and some time to plan my future. What do I want to do? I could apply to join a fire crew at an airport.

I could specialize in fighting forest fires, but I'd have to leave the city. If I stay where I am, I might be put in charge of a group of firefighters. One day I could become a station manager.

Writing a diary

Firefighters at the **fire station** keep a log of everything that happens. The log **records** the time and reason that each fire engine is called out. This book is a diary. It tells what happened from the firefighter's point of view.

You can write a diary too! Your diary can describe your life – what you saw, what you felt, and the events that happened.

Here are some tips for writing a diary:

- Start each entry with the day and the date. You don't have to include an entry for every day.

- The entries should be in **chronological** order, which means that they follow the order in which events happened.

- Use the past tense when you are writing about something that has already happened.

- Remember that a diary is the writer's story, so use "I" and "my".

Glossary

breathing apparatus mask, pipe, and supply of air

casualties people hurt in an accident

chemicals solids, liquids, or gases that are used to make something. Some chemicals are harmful.

chronological in order of time

cordoned off closed to the public by a length of tape, or a barrier

fire door door that does not burn easily and so helps to stop a fire from spreading

fire drill set of actions to do with fire safety that are repeated again and again

fire exit way out of a building if there is a fire

fire resistant does not catch fire

fire station building where fire engines and equipment are kept and where firefighters work and stay when on duty

good head for heights able to be high above the ground without feeling dizzy or scared

hazard suit special clothes worn for dealing with something dangerous

record write something down for later use

recruit someone who has only just joined the fire service

siren machine that makes a loud noise to catch people's attention

smoke alarm device that beeps very loudly when smoke reaches it

Find out more

Books

At the Fire Station (Helping Hands), Ruth Thomson (Wayland, 2008)

Fire Engines (Look and Play), Jim Pipe (Franklin Watts, 2008)

Firefighters (People Who Help Us), Clare Oliver (Franklin Watts, 2006)

Firefighters, Katie Daynes (Usborne Beginners, 2007)

Websites

www.cambsfire.gov.uk/interactivezone.php
A website for children created by the Cambridgeshire Fire and Rescue Service. It has interactive sections for children of all ages.

www.fire.nsw.gov.au/page.php?id=210
Click on Schools and then Brigade Kids to go to a website for children. There you can choose to see around a fire station or find out what is inside each part of a fire engine – and lots more!

www.firefacts.org/
Click on Kids Club to get entry to Club Firefacts where you can find information about safety, games, and other fun stuff.

Index